GW01159388

Spanish Short Stories for Beginners
Book 1

Over 100 Dialogues and Daily Used Phrases to Learn Spanish in Your Car. Have Fun & Grow Your Vocabulary, with Crazy Effective Language Learning Lessons

www.LearnLikeNatives.com

TABLE OF CONTENT

INTRODUCTION

B efore we dive into some Spanish, I want to congratulate you, whether you're just beginning, continuing, or resuming your language learning journey. Here at Learn Like a Native, we understand the determination it takes to pick up a new language and after reading this book, you'll be another step closer to achieving your language goals.

As a thank you for learning with us, we are giving you free access to our 'Speak Like a Native' eBook. It's packed full of practical advice and insider tips on how to make language learning quick, easy, and most importantly, enjoyable. Head over to LearnLikeNatives.com to access your free guide and peruse our huge selection of language learning resources.

Learning a new language is a bit like cooking—you need several different ingredients and the right technique, but the end result is sure to be delicious. We created this book of short stories for learning Spanish because language is alive. Language is about the senses—hearing, tasting the words on your tongue, and touching another culture up close. Learning a language in a classroom is a fine place to start, but it's not a complete introduction to a language.

In this book, you'll find a language come to life. These short stories are miniature immersions into the Spanish language, at a level that is perfect for beginners. This book is not a lecture on grammar. It's not an endless vocabulary list. This book is the closest you can come to a language immersion without leaving the country. In the stories within, you will see people speaking to each other, going through daily life situations, and using the most common, helpful words and phrases in language.

You are holding the key to bringing your Spanish studies to life.

Made for Beginners

We made this book with beginners in mind. You'll find that the language is simple, but not boring. Most of the book is in the present tense, so you will be able to focus on dialogues, root verbs, and understand and find patterns in subject-verb agreement.

This is not "just" a translated book. While reading novels and short stories translated into Spanish is a wonderful thing, beginners (and even novices) often run into difficulty. Literary licenses and complex sentence structure can make reading in your second language truly difficult—not to mention BORING. That's why Spanish Short

Stories for Beginners is the perfect book to pick up. The stories are simple, but not infantile. They were not written for children, but the language is simple so that beginners can pick it up.

The Benefits of Learning a Second Language

If you have picked up this book, it's likely that you are already aware of the many benefits of learning a second language. Besides just being fun, knowing more than one language opens up a whole new world to you. You will be able to communicate with a much larger chunk of the world. Opportunities in the workforce will open up, and maybe even your day-to-day work will be improved. Improved communication can also help you expand your business. And from a neurological perspective, learning a second language is like taking your daily vitamins and eating well, for your brain!

How To Use The Book

The chapters of this book all follow the same structure:

- A short story with several dialogs
- A summary in Spanish
- A list of important words and phrases and their English translation
- Questions to test your understanding
- Answers to check if you were right
- The English translation of the story to clear every doubt

You may use this book however is comfortable for you, but we have a few recommendations for getting the most out of the experience. Try these tips and if they work for you, you can use them on every chapter throughout the book.

1) Start by reading the story all the way through. Don't stop or get hung up on any particular words or phrases. See how much of the plot you can understand in this way. We think you'll get a lot more of it than you may expect, but it is completely normal not to understand everything in the story. You are learning a new language, and that takes time.

2) Read the summary in Spanish. See if it matches what you have understood of the plot.

3) Read the story through again, slower this time. See if you can pick up the meaning of any words or phrases you don't understand by using context clues and the information from the summary.

4) Test yourself! Try to answer the five comprehension questions that come at the end of each story. Write your answers down, and then check them against the answer key. How did you do? If you didn't get them all, no worries!

5) Look over the vocabulary list that accompanies the chapter. Are any of these the words you did not understand? Did you already know the meaning of some of them from your reading?

6) Now go through the story once more. Pay attention this time to the words and phrases you haven't understand. If you'd like, take the time to look them up to

expand your meaning of the story. Every time you read over the story, you'll understand more and more.

7) Move on to the next chapter when you are ready.

Read and Listen

The audio version is the best way to experience this book, as you will hear a native Spanish speaker tell you each story. You will become accustomed to their accent as you listen along, a huge plus for when you want to apply your new language skills in the real world.

If this has ignited your language learning passion and you are keen to find out what other resources are available, go to **LearnLikeNatives.com**, where you can access our vast range of free learning materials. Don't know where to begin? An excellent place to start is our 'Speak Like a Native' free eBook, full of practical advice and insider tips on how to make language learning quick, easy, and most importantly, enjoyable.

And remember, small steps add up to great advancements! No moment is better to begin learning than the present.

FREE BOOK!

Get the *FREE BOOK* that reveals the secrets path to learn any language fast, and without leaving your country.

Discover:

- The **language 5 golden rules** to master languages at will

- Proven **mind training techniques** to revolutionize your learning

- A complete step-by-step guide to **conquering any language**

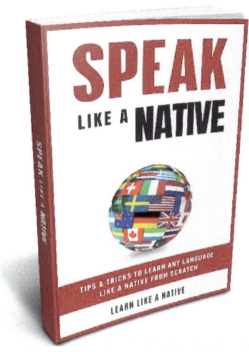

CHAPTER 1
The Mysterious Package / Greetings

Suena el timbre de la puerta.

Andrew corre a la puerta del apartamento. El timbre nunca suena los sábados por la mañana. Andrew está emocionado de ver quién está en la puerta. Él abre la puerta.

"Buenos días, niño", dice un repartidor. El hombre está vestido con un uniforme marrón y lleva una caja marrón.

"Hola, señor", dice Andrew.

"Tengo un paquete", dice el repartidor. "Dice Calle Principal Nº10."

"Esta es la Calle Principal Nº10", dice Andrew.

"El paquete no tiene nombre", dice el repartidor. "Tampoco tiene número de apartamento."

"¡Qué extraño!", dice Andrew.

"¿Puedes dárselo a la persona correcta?", pregunta el hombre.

"Puedo intentarlo", dice Andrew. Sólo tiene diez años, pero se siente importante.

"**Muchas gracias**", dice el repartidor. Se va. Andrew lleva la caja a su casa. La mira. Es aproximadamente del tamaño de una caja de zapatos. No tiene nombre en el exterior, sólo Calle Principal Nº10.

Andrew abre la caja de cartón. Necesita saber qué hay dentro para encontrar al dueño. Hay una pequeña caja de madera dentro de la caja de cartón. Andrew abre la caja de madera. Dentro de la caja hay 10 pares diferentes de gafas. Son de diferentes colores: rosa y rojo, de puntos verdes, blanco y negro. También son de diferentes formas: redondas, cuadradas y rectangulares.

Cierra la caja y se pone los zapatos.

"¡**Adiós** mamá! Vuelvo enseguida", grita.

Andrew llama a la puerta al otro lado del pasillo de su casa. Se abre. Una señora muy anciana le sonríe a Andrew y la caja.

"¡**Buenos días**, Sra. Smith!", dice Andrew.

"**¿Cómo estás?**", pregunta la anciana.

"Bien, ¡gracias! ¿Y usted?", dice Andrew.

"¿Qué pasa?", pregunta la anciana.

"Señora, esto es un paquete. Pertenece a alguien de este edificio, pero no sé de quién es", dice Andrew.

"No es para mí", dice la anciana. "¡Imposible!"

"Oh, ok" dice Andrew, decepcionado. La anciana lleva gafas. Él piensa que estas gafas se verían bien en ella. Se da la vuelta para irse.

"Vuelve más tarde", dice a la anciana. "Estoy haciendo galletas y algunas son para ti y tu familia."

Andrew sube las escaleras. Su edificio tiene tres pisos. Es amigo de casi todos en el edificio. Sin embargo, en el apartamento del segundo piso hay una nueva familia. Andrew no los conoce. Se siente tímido, pero toca la campana. Un hombre de pelo castaño abre la puerta. Sonríe.

"¡**Hola**!", dice el hombre.

"**Hola**", dice Andrew. "Vivo abajo. **Mi nombre es** Andrew."

"**Es un placer conocerte**, Andrew", dice el hombre. "Somos nuevos en el edificio. Soy el Sr. Jones."

"**Encantado de conocerlo también**", dice Andrew. "Este paquete pertenece a alguien de este edificio. ¿Es suyo este paquete?"

"¡Imposible!", dice el hombre. "Mi familia y yo acabamos de mudarnos aquí. Nadie sabe nuestra dirección."

"Ok," dice Andrew. "Encantado de conocerte entonces." La puerta se cierra. Otro no. Sólo hay dos apartamentos para probar. En el siguiente apartamento hay una familia. La hija va a la misma escuela que Andrew. Ella es un año mayor que Andrew. Su nombre es Diana. Andrew piensa que ella es muy hermosa. Él se vuelve a sentir tímido otra vez, pero igualmente llama a la puerta.

Una chica guapa y rubia abre la puerta.

Hola, Diana, sonríe Andrew.

"**¿Qué pasa?**" dice Diana. Lleva pijamas de color rosa brillante y su pelo está desordenado.

"**¿Cómo te va?**", pregunta Andrew.

"Todo bien", dice Diana. "Estaba dormida. Me despertaste."

"Lo siento", él dice rápidamente. Su cara se enrojeció. Se siente muy avergonzado. "Tengo un paquete. No sabemos a quién pertenece."

"¿Qué hay en él?", pregunta Diana.

"Algunas gafas. Son gafas para leer", dice Andrew.

"No uso gafas. Mi mamá no las usa. La caja no es para nosotras", dice Diana.

"Ok", dice Andrew. Se despide y sube las escaleras. Hay un apartamento más, el apartamento en el tercer piso. El Sr. Edwards vive solo en ese apartamento. Tiene un gran loro que sabe hablar. También tiene cuatro gatos y un perro. Su apartamento es viejo y oscuro. Andrew tiene miedo del Sr. Edwards. Toca el timbre. Tiene que averiguar a quién pertenece la caja.

"**Hola**", dice el Sr. Edwards. Su perro llega a la puerta. El perro ayuda al Sr. Edwards porque es ciego.

"Hola, Sr. Edwards. Soy Andrew", dice Andrew. El Sr. Edwards tiene los ojos cerrados. Sonríe.

"¿**Qué hay de nuevo**, Andrew?" Pregunta. Hmmm, piensa Andrew, quizás el Sr. Edwards no da miedo. Quizás el Sr. Edwards es sólo un agradable anciano que vive solo.

"Tengo un paquete y creo que es para usted", dice Andrew.

¡Ah sí! Mis gafas de lectura. ¡Finalmente!" sonríe el Sr. Edwards. Extiende sus manos. Andrew está confundido. Mira al perro. Parece estar sonriendo, también. Le da la caja al Sr. Edwards.

"Qué bueno verte", dice el Sr. Edwards.

"Igualmente", dice Andrew. Quizás visite al Sr. Edwards otro día. Se da la vuelta y se va a casa.

RESUMEN

Un niño, Andrew, recibe un paquete que no es para él. Es una caja con gafas. Se lo lleva a los vecinos, uno por uno, para averiguar a quién pertenece el paquete. Descubre que el paquete pertenece a su vecino, el Sr. Edwards, lo que es un poco sorprendente.

Lista de Vocabulario

Good morning	Buenos días
Hello	Hola
Sir	Señor
Thank you very much	Muchas gracias
Bye	Adiós
Morning!	Buen día
How are you?	¿Cómo estás?
Fine, thanks!	¡Bien, gracias!
And you?	¿Y tú? / ¿Y usted?
Ma'am	Señora
Hi	Hola
My name is...	Mi nombre es...
It's nice to meet you	Es un placer conocerte
Nice to meet you too	Encantado de conocerte también

How's it going?	¿Qué tal te va?
It's going	Todo bien
Hey	Hey
What's up	Qué pasa
What's new	Qué hay de nuevo
It's good to see you	Me alegro de verte

PREGUNTAS

1. ¿Quién está en la puerta principal cuando Andrew lo abre?

    a) un repartidor

    b) un gato

    c) un censista

    d) su padre

2. ¿Cómo describiría a la Sra. Smith?

    a) una chica hermosa

    b) una persona desagradable

    c) un mal vecino

    d) una buena anciana

3. ¿Quién vive en el segundo piso del edificio?

    a) nadie

b) una chica de la escuela de Andrew

c) una nueva familia

d) Andrew

4. ¿Cómo crees que se siente Andrew con Diana?

a) le gusta y piensa que es bonita

b) la sigue en las redes sociales

c) no le gusta

d) no se conocen

5. ¿A quién pertenecen las gafas en el edificio?

a) la anciana

b) el hombre ciego

c) Andrew y su familia

d) nadie

RESPUESTAS

1. ¿Quién está en la puerta principal cuando Andrew lo abre?

    a) un repartidor

2. ¿Cómo describiría a la Sra. Smith?

    d) una buena anciana

3. ¿Quién vive en el segundo piso del edificio de apartamentos?

    c) una nueva familia

4. ¿Cómo crees que se siente Andrew con Diana?

    a) le gusta y piensa que es bonita

5. ¿A quién pertenecen las gafas en el edificio de apartamentos?

b) el hombre ciego

Translation of the Story

The Mysterious Package

The doorbell rings.

Andrew runs to the door of the apartment. The doorbell never rings on Saturday mornings. Andrew is excited to see who is at the door. He opens the door.

"**Good morning**, little boy," says a delivery man. The man is dressed in a brown uniform and is carrying a brown box.

"**Hello**, **sir**," says Andrew.

"I have a package," the delivery man says. "It says 10 Main Street."

"This is 10 Main Street," says Andrew.

"The package has no name," says the delivery man. "It also has no apartment number."

"How strange!" says Andrew.

"Can you give it to the right person?" the man asks.

"I can try," says Andrew. He is only ten years old, but he feels important.

"Thank you very much," says the delivery man. He leaves. Andrew takes the box into his house. He stares at the box. It is about the size of a shoe box. It has no name on the outside, just 10 Main Street.

Andrew opens the cardboard box. He needs to know what is inside to find the owner. There is a small wood box inside the cardboard box. Andrew opens the wooden box. Inside the box are 10 different pairs of eyeglasses. They are different colors: pink and red, green polka dots, black and white. They are also different shapes: round, square and rectangle.

He closes the box and puts on his shoes.

"**Bye** mom! I'll be right back," he shouts.

Andrew knocks on the door across the hall from his house. It opens. A very old lady smiles at Andrew and the box.

"**Morning**, Mrs. Smith!" says Andrew.

"How are you?" asks the old lady.

"Fine, thanks! And you?" says Andrew.

"What do you have?" asks the old lady.

"Ma'am, this is a package. It belongs to someone in this building but I don't know who," says Andrew.

"It's not for me," says the old lady. "Impossible!"

"Oh, ok" says Andrew, disappointed. The old lady wears glasses. He thinks these glasses would look nice on her. He turns to leave.

"Come back later," calls the old lady. "I'm making cookies and some cookies are for you and your family."

Andrew goes up the stairs. His building has three floors. He is friends with almost everyone in the building. However, the apartment on the second floor has a new family. Andrew doesn't know them. He feels shy, but he rings the bell. A brown-haired man opens the door. He smiles.

"Hi!" says the man.

"Hello," says Andrew. "I live downstairs. **My name is** Andrew."

"It's nice to meet you, Andrew," the man says. "We are new to the building. I'm Mr. Jones."

"Nice to meet you too," says Andrew. "This package belongs to someone in this building. Is it your package?"

"Impossible!" says the man. "My family and I just moved here. No one knows our address."

"Ok," says Andrew. "Nice to meet you then." The door closes. Another no. There are only two apartments left to try. In the next apartment is a family. The daughter goes to the same school as Andrew. She is a year older than Andrew. Her name is Diana. Andrew thinks she is very beautiful. He feels shy again, but he knocks on the door.

A pretty, blonde girl opens the door.

"Hey, Diana," Andrew smiles.

"What's up?" Diana says. Her pijamas are bright pink and her hair is messy.

"How's it going?" Andrew asks.

"It's going," Diana says. "I was asleep. You woke me up."

"I'm sorry," he says quickly. His face is red. He feels extra shy. "I have a package. We don't know who it belongs to."

"What is in it?" asks Diana.

"Some glasses. They are glasses for reading," says Andrew.

"I don't wear glasses. My mom doesn't use them. The box is not for us," says Diana.

"Ok," says Andrew. He waves goodbye and climbs the stairs. There is one more apartment, the apartment on the third floor. Mr. Edwards lives in this apartment, alone. He has a big parrot that knows how to talk. He also has four cats and a dog. His apartment is old and dark. Andrew feels afraid of Mr. Edwards. He rings the doorbell. He has to find out who the box belongs to.

"Hello," says Mr. Edwards. His dog comes to the door. The dog helps Mr. Edwards because he is blind.

"Hi, Mr. Edwards. It's Andrew," Andrew says. Mr. Edwards has his eyes closed. He smiles.

"What's new, Andrew?" He asks. Hmmm, Andrew thinks, maybe Mr. Edwards isn't scary. Maybe Mr. Edwards is just a nice old man that lives alone.

"I have a package and I think it is for you," says Andrew.

"Ah yes! My reading glasses. Finally!" smiles Mr. Edwards. He holds his hands out. Andrew is confused. He looks at the dog. It seems to be smiling, too. He gives Mr. Edwards the box.

"It's good to see you," says Mr. Edwards.

"You too," says Andrew. Maybe he will visit Mr. Edwards another day. He turns around and goes home.

CHAPTER 2
Mardi Gras /

Colors + Days of the Week

HISTORIA

Frank sale por la puerta principal. Su nueva casa es **violeta** con ventanas azules. Los colores son muy brillantes para una casa. En Nueva Orleans, su nuevo hogar, los edificios son coloridos.

Es nuevo en el barrio. Frank todavía no tiene amigos. La casa a su lado es un edificio alto y **rojo**. Allí vive una familia. Frank mira fijamente a la puerta, y un hombre la abre. Frank dice hola.

"¡Hola, vecino!", dice George. Él saluda. Frank camina hacia la casa roja.

"Hola, soy Frank, el nuevo vecino", dice Frank.

Encantado de conocerte. Mi nombre es George, dice George. Los hombres se dan la mano. George tiene una cadena de luces en sus manos. Las luces son **verdes**, **moradas** y **doradas**.

"¿Para qué son las luces?", pregunta Frank.

"Eres nuevo", se ríe George. "Es Mardi Gras, ¿no lo sabías? Estos colores representan las fiestas del carnaval aquí en Nueva Orleans."

"Oh, sí", dice Frank. Frank no sabe del carnaval. Tampoco tiene amigos con quienes hacer planes.

"Hoy es **viernes**", dice George. "Hay un desfile llamado Endymion. ¿Vendrás conmigo y la familia a verlo?"

"Sí", dice Frank. "¡Maravilloso!"

George pone las luces en la casa. Frank ayuda a George. George enciende las luces. La casa se ve festiva.

La familia y Frank van al desfile. Durante el Mardi Gras en Nueva Orleáns, hay desfiles todos los días. Los desfiles de la **semana** son pequeños. Los desfiles del fin de semana, **sábado** y **domingo**, son grandes, con muchas carrozas y personas. Hay un rey del Mardi Gras. Su nombre es Rex.

Mardi Gras significa "**Martes** de grasa". En Inglaterra, se llama Martes de Carnaval. La fiesta es católica. Es un día antes del **Miércoles** de Ceniza, el comienzo de la Cuaresma. El Mardi Gras es la celebración antes de la Cuaresma, es un momento muy serio. Para el jueves, los días especiales han terminado. Nueva Orleans es famosa por su carnaval. La gente tiene fiestas y usan máscaras y disfraces. De hecho, sólo se puede usar una máscara en Nueva Orleans en Mardi Gras. ¡El resto del año es ilegal!

George y su familia ven el desfile comenzar con Frank. Frank está sorprendido. Hay mucha gente mirando. Ellos están de pie en la hierba. Las carrozas pasan el grupo. Las carrozas son grandes estructuras con gente y decoraciones. Bajan por la calle, una por una.

El primer flotador representa el sol. Tiene decoraciones **amarillas**. Una mujer en el medio lleva un vestido **blanco**. Se ve como un ángel. Ella lanza juguetes **naranjas** y collares a la gente.

"¿Por qué tira los juguetes y los collares?", pregunta Frank.

"¡Para nosotros!", dice Hannah, la esposa de George. Hannah sostiene cinco collares en sus manos. Algunos collares están en el suelo. Nadie los atrapa. Están sucios y son **marrones**.

El desfile continúa. Hay muchas carrozas, y muchos collares. George y su familia gritan, "¡Tírame algo, señor!" Hannah llena su bolso **negro** con coloridos juguetes y collares de las carrozas. Frank aprende a gritar "¡Tírame algo!" para conseguir collares para sí mismo.

Una gran carroza tiene más de 250 personas en ella. Es la más grande del mundo.

Finalmente, el desfile termina. Los niños y los adultos son felices. Todos se van a casa. Frank está cansado. También tiene hambre y quiere comer. Sigue a George y a su familia hasta la casa **roja**. Hay una gran tarta redonda sobre la mesa. Parece un anillo, con un agujero en el medio. El pastel tiene un glaseado **morado**, **verde** y **amarillo** en la parte superior.

"Esto es pastel rey", dice Hannah. "Comemos pastel rey cada Mardi Gras."

Hannah corta un pedazo de pastel. Ella le da un pedazo a George, un pedazo a los niños, y un pedazo a Frank. Frank prueba el pastel. ¡Es delicioso! Sabe a canela. Es suave. Pero de repente Frank muerde el plástico.

"¡Ay!" dice Frank. Frank deja de comer. Saca un bebé de plástico del pastel.

"Hay una tradición más", dice George. "El pastel tiene un bebé en él. La persona que recibe el bebé compra el siguiente pastel."

"¡Ese soy yo!", dice Frank.

Todos se ríen. George invita a Frank a otro desfile el **lunes**.

Frank se va a casa feliz. Le encanta el Mardi Gras.

Lista de Vocabulario

violet	violeta
blue	azul
colors	colores
red	rojo
green	verde
purple	púrpura
gold	dorado
Friday	Viernes
week	semana
Saturday	Sábado
Sunday	Domingo
Tuesday	Martes
Wednesday	Miércoles

Thursday	Jueves
yellow	amarillo
white	blanco
orange	naranja
brown	marrón
black	negro
Monday	Lunes

PREGUNTAS

1) ¿Cómo describiría la nueva casa de Frank?

    a) aburrida

    b) colorida

    c) pequeña

    d) solitaria

2) ¿Qué color representa el Mardi Gras en Nueva Orleans?

    a) azul

    b) blanco

    c) naranja

    d) dorado

3) El Mardi Gras es una celebración:

    a) sólo para adultos.

    b) de la tradición de la iglesia judía.

    c) famosa en Nueva Orleans.

    d) que se hace dentro de una casa.

4) ¿Cuál de estos no está en una carroza de Mardi Gras?

    a) personas

    b) computadoras

c) juguetes

d) collares

5) ¿Qué pasa si encuentras al bebé en un pastel rey?

a) lloras

b) debes cuidar del bebé

c) se lo das a tu amigo

d) debes comprar una torta rey

RESPUESTAS

1) ¿Cómo describiría la nueva casa de Frank?

   a) aburrida

2) ¿Qué color representa el Mardi Gras en Nueva Orleans?

   d) dorado

3) El Mardi Gras es una celebración:

   c) famosa en Nueva Orleans.

4) ¿Cuál de ellos no está en una carroza de Mardi Gras?

   b) computadoras

5) ¿Qué pasa si encuentras al bebé en un pastel rey?

d) debes comprar una torta rey

Translation of the Story

Mardi Gras

STORY

Frank steps out his front door. His new house is **violet** with **blue** windows. The **colors** are very bright for a house. In New Orleans, his new home, buildings are colorful.

He is new to the neighborhood. Frank does not have any friends yet. The house next to him is a tall, **red** building. A family lives there. Frank stares at the door, and a man opens it. Frank says hello.

"Hello, neighbor!" says George. He waves. Frank walks to the red house.

"Hi, I'm Frank, the new neighbor," says Frank.

"Nice to meet you. My name is George," George says. The men shake hands. George has a string of lights in his hands. The lights are **green**, **purple** and **gold**.

"What are the lights for?" asks Frank.

"You *are* new," laughs George. "It's Mardi Gras, didn't you know? These colors represent the holiday of carnival here in New Orleans."

"Oh, yes," says Frank. Frank does not know about carnival. He also has no friends to make plans with.

"Today is **Friday**," says George. "There is a parade called Endymion. Will you come with me and the family to watch?"

"Yes," Frank says. "Wonderful!"

George puts the lights on the house. Frank helps George. George turns on the lights. The house looks festive.

The family and Frank go to the parade. During Mardi Gras in New Orleans, there are parades every day. The parades during the **week** are small. The parades on the weekend, **Saturday** and **Sunday**, are big, with many floats and people. There is a king of Mardi Gras. His name is Rex.

Mardi Gras means 'Fat **Tuesday'.** In England, it is called Shrove Tuesday. The holiday is Catholic. It is one day before Ash **Wednesday**, the beginning of Lent. Mardi Gras is the celebration before Lent, a serious time. By **Thursday**, the special days are finished. New Orleans is famous for its Mardi Gras. People have parties and wear masks and costumes. In fact, you can only wear a mask in New Orleans on Mardi Gras. The rest of the year it is illegal!

George and his family watch the parade begin with Frank. Frank is surprised. There are many people watching. They stand in the grass. Floats pass the group. Floats are big structures with people and decorations. They go down the street, one by one.

The first float represents the sun. It has **yellow** decorations. A woman in the middle wears a **white** dress. She looks like an angel. She throws **orange** toys and beads to the people.

58

"Why does she throw the toys and necklaces?" asks Frank.

"For us!" says Hannah, George's wife. Hannah holds five necklaces in her hands. Some beads are on the ground. Nobody catches them. They are dirty and **brown**.

The parade continues. There are many floats, and many beads. George and his family shout, "Throw me something, mister!" Hannah fills her **black** bag with colorful toys and beads from the floats. Frank learns to shout "Throw me something!" to get beads for himself.

One big float has over 250 people on it. It is the largest in the world.

Finally, the parade ends. The children and the adults are happy. Everyone goes home. Frank is tired. He is also hungry and wants to eat. He follows George and his family into the **red** house. There is a big, round cake on the table. It looks like a ring, with a hole in the middle. The cake has **purple**, **green** and **yellow** frosting on top.

"This is king cake," Hannah says. "We eat king cake every Mardi Gras."

Hannah cuts a piece of cake. She gives one piece to George, one piece to the children, and one piece to Frank. Frank tastes the cake. It is delicious! It tastes like cinnamon. It is soft. But suddenly Frank bites into plastic.

"Ouch!" says Frank. Frank stops eating. He pulls a plastic baby out of the cake.

"There is one more tradition," says George. "The cake has a baby in it. The person who gets the baby buys the next cake."

"That's me!" Frank says.

Everyone laughs. George invites Frank to another parade on **Monday.**

Frank goes home happy. He loves Mardi Gras.

CHAPTER 3
Weird Weather / Weather

HISTORIA

Ivan tiene doce años. Visita a sus abuelos el fin de semana. Le encanta visitar a sus abuelos. La abuela le da galletas y leche todos los días. El abuelo le enseña cosas interesantes. Este fin de semana va a su casa.

Es febrero. Donde está Iván, es **invierno**. En febrero suele **nevar**. A Iván le encanta la nieve. Juega en ella y la hace rodar bolas de nieve. Este fin de semana de febrero, el **clima** es diferente. El sol brilla; está **soleado** y muy **caliente** ¿Ivan lleva una camiseta a la casa de su abuelo.

"¡Hola, abuelo! ¡Hola, abuela!" dice Ivan.

"¡Hola, Ivan!" dice la abuela.

"¡Iván! ¿Cómo estás?", dice el abuelo.

"Estoy bien", dice, y abraza a sus abuelos. Ivan se despide de su madre.

Entran en la casa. "Este clima es extraño", dice la abuela. "febrero es siempre **frío** y **nublado**. ¡No entiendo!"

"Es el **cambio climático**", dice Ivan. En la escuela, Ivan aprende sobre la contaminación. El clima varía debido a los cambios en la atmósfera. El cambio climático es la diferencia en el tiempo.

"No sé sobre el cambio climático", dice el abuelo. "**Predigo** el clima por lo que veo."

"¿Qué quieres decir?", pregunta Ivan.

"Esta mañana, el **cielo** es rojo", dice el abuelo. "Esto significa que sé que una tormenta se avecina."

"¿Cómo?", pregunta Ivan.

"Cielo rojo por la mañana, los marineros toman advertencia. Cielo rojo por la noche, placer de los marineros." El abuelo le dice a Iván acerca de este dicho.

Si el cielo es rojo al amanecer, significa que hay agua en el aire. La luz del sol brilla de color rojo. La tormenta viene hacia ustedes. Si el cielo es rojo al atardecer, el mal tiempo se va. Sin **meteorólogos**, la gente mira el cielo en busca de pistas sobre el clima.

"¿Cómo predicen los meteorólogos el clima?", pregunta Iván.

"Miran los patrones en la atmósfera", dice la abuela. "Miran la temperatura, si es caliente o fría. Y miran la presión del aire, lo que está sucediendo en la atmósfera."

"Predigo el clima de manera diferente", dice el abuelo. "Por ejemplo, sé que hoy lloverá."

"¿Cómo?", pregunta Ivan.

"El gato", dice el abuelo. Ivan mira al gato. El gato abre su boca y dice "ah-chuu".

"Cuando el gato estornuda o ronca, eso significa que viene la lluvia", dice el abuelo. Puede **lloviznar** o puede ser muy **lluvioso**, pero lloverá."

De repente, escuchan un fuerte sonido. Ivan mira por la ventana. Las gotas de lluvia caen con fuerza. La lluvia es fuerte. Ivan no puede escuchar lo que dice su abuelo.

"¿Qué?" dice Ivan

"Está **lloviendo gatos y perros**", dice el abuelo, sonriendo.

"¡ah!" ríe Ivan

"Sé otra forma de saber el clima", dice la abuela.

La abuela mira a las arañas para ver cuándo hará frío. Al final del **verano**, el clima cambia. El **otoño** trae brisa fresca. La abuela sabe que cuando las arañas entran, significa que viene el clima frío. Las arañas hacen una casa adentro antes del invierno. Así es como la abuela sabe cuándo llega el clima invernal.

La lluvia se detiene. El abuelo e Ivan salen. El abuelo y la abuela viven en una casa en el bosque. La casa tiene árboles a su alrededor. Es una casa pequeña. Ivan tiene frío con su camiseta. El clima no es soleado. El aire se mueve. Hace **viento**. El viento sopla a través del cabello de Ivan.

"Hace **frío** ahora", dice Ivan.

"Sí", dice el abuelo. "¿Cuál es la temperatura?"

"No lo sé", dice Ivan. "No tengo un termómetro".

"No necesitas uno", dice el abuelo. El abuelo le dice a Ivan que escuche. Ivan oye un sonido: *cri-cri-cri*. Es un insecto. El *cri-cri-cri* es el sonido de los grillos. El abuelo le enseña a Ivan. Ivan cuenta el *cri* durante catorce segundos. El abuelo suma 40 a ese número. Esa es la temperatura afuera. Ivan no sabía que los grillos eran como termómetros.

La abuela sale de la casa. Ella sonríe. Mira a Ivan contando el sonido del *cri*. "¡Hora de galletas y leche!" ella dice.

"¡Hurra!" dice Ivan

"¡Oh mira!" dice la abuela. "Es un arcoíris". El arcoíris va de la casa al bosque. Tiene muchos colores: rojo, naranja, amarillo, azul y verde. El arcoíris es hermoso. La abuela, el abuelo e Ivan miran el arcoíris. Desaparece y entran.

"Galletas y leche para todos", dice la abuela. Ella le da a Ivan una galleta de chocolate caliente.

"No para mí", dice el abuelo. "Quiero té."

"¿Por qué el té?" dice la abuela. Ella tiene dos leches en la mano.

"Me siento con **mal tiempo**", dice el abuelo. Él ríe. Ivan y la abuela se ríen con él.

Lista de Vocabulario

winter	invierno
to snow	nevar
weather	clima
sunny	soleado
hot	caliente
cold	frío
cloudy	nublado
climate change	cambio climático
atmosphere	atmosfera
predict	predecir
sky	cielo
storm	tormenta
weathermen	meteorólogo
drizzle	llovizna
rainy	lluvioso

raining cats and dogs	lloviendo gatos y perros
summer	verano
autumn	otoño
windy	ventoso
temperature	temperatura
thermometer	termómetro
rainbow	arcoíris
under the weather	mal tiempo

PREGUNTAS

1) ¿Cómo suele ser el tiempo en febrero?

   a) caliente

   b) frío

   c) soleado

   d) fresco

2) ¿Cómo sabe el abuelo cómo será el clima?

   a) ve la televisión

   b) los meteorólogos

   c) observa la naturaleza

   d) no predice el tiempo

3) ¿Qué significa llover gatos y perros?

   a) la lluvia moja a los gatos

b) está lloviendo sólo un poco

c) gatos y perros caen del cielo

d) está lloviendo muy fuerte

4) ¿Qué significa cuando las arañas entran?

a) tienen hambre

b) están listas para poner huevos

c) el clima frío se acerca

d) el clima cálido se acerca

5) ¿Por qué el abuelo pide té en lugar de leche?

a) se siente un poco enfermo

b) es alérgico a la leche

c) quiere una bebida caliente

d) hacer enojar a la abuela

RESPUESTAS

1) ¿Cómo suele ser el tiempo en febrero?

    a) caliente

2) ¿Cómo sabe el abuelo cómo será el clima?

    c) observa la naturaleza

3) ¿Qué significa llover gatos y perros?

    d) está lloviendo muy fuerte

4) ¿Qué significa cuando las arañas entran?

    c) el clima frío se acerca

5) ¿Por qué el abuelo pide té en lugar de leche?

    a) se siente un poco enfermo

Translation of the Story

Weird Weather

STORY

Ivan is twelve years old. He visits his grandparents on the weekend. He loves to visit his grandparents. Grandma gives him cookies and milk every day. Grandpa teaches him neat things. This weekend he goes to their house.

It is February. Where Ivan is, it is **winter**. In February, it usually **snows**. Ivan loves the snow. He plays in it and rolls it into balls. This February weekend, the **weather** is different. The sun is shining; it is **sunny** and almost **hot**! Ivan wears a T-shirt to his grandparent's house.

"Hi, Grandpa! Hi, Grandma!" Ivan says.

"Hello, Ivan!" Grandma says.

"Ivan! How are you?" says Grandpa.

"I'm good," he says, and he hugs his grandparents. Ivan says goodbye to his mom.

They go into the house. "This weather is strange," says Grandma. "February is always **cold** and **cloudy**. I don't understand!"

"It is **climate change**," says Ivan. In school, Ivan learns about contamination and pollution. The weather changes because of changes in the **atmosphere**. Climate change is the difference in the weather over time.

"I don't know about climate change," says Grandpa. "I **predict** the weather by what I see."

"What do you mean?" asks Ivan.

"This morning, the **sky** is red," says Grandpa. "This means I know a **storm** is coming."

"How?" asks Ivan.

"Red sky in the morning, sailors take warning. Red sky at night, sailor's delight." Grandpa tells Ivan about this saying.

If the sky is red at sunrise, it means there is water in the air. The light of the sun shines red. The storm is coming towards you. If the sky is red at sunset, the bad weather is leaving. Without **weathermen**, people watch the sky for clues about the weather.

"How do weathermen predict the weather?" asks Ivan.

"They look at patterns in the atmosphere," says Grandma. "They look at temperature, if it is hot or cold. And they look at air pressure, what is happening in the atmosphere."

"I predict the weather differently," says Grandpa. "For example, I know today it will **rain**."

"How?" asks Ivan.

"The cat," says Grandpa. Ivan looks at the cat. The cat opens its mouth and says 'ah-CHOO'.

"When the cat sneezes or snores, that means rain is coming," says Grandpa. It may **drizzle** or it may be very **rainy**, but it will rain."

Suddenly, they hear a loud sound. Ivan looks out the window. Drops of rain are falling hard. The rain is loud. Ivan can't hear what his Grandpa says.

"What?" says Ivan.

"It's **raining cats and dogs,**" says Grandpa, smiling.

"Ha!" laughs Ivan.

"I know another way to tell the weather," says Grandma.

Grandma watches the spiders to see when the weather will be cold. At the end of **summer**, the weather changes. **Autumn** brings fresh, cool air. Grandma knows that when spiders come inside, it means cold weather is coming. The spiders make a house inside before winter. That is how grandma knows when the winter weather comes.

The rain stops. Grandpa and Ivan go out. Grandpa and Grandma live in a house in the forest. The house has trees around it. It is a small house. Ivan is cold in his T-shirt. The weather is not sunny. The air is moving. It is **windy**. The wind blows through Ivan's hair.

"It is **cold** now," says Ivan.

"Yes," says Grandpa. "What is the temperature?"

"I don't know," says Ivan. "I don't have a thermometer."

"You don't need one," says Grandpa. Grandpa tells Ivan to listen. Ivan hears a sound: *cri-cri-cri*. It is an insect. The *cri-cri-cri* is the sound of crickets. Grandpa teaches Ivan. Ivan counts the *cri* for fourteen seconds. Grandpa adds 40 to that number. That is the temperature outside. Ivan did not know crickets were like thermometers.

Grandma comes out of the house. She smiles. She watches Ivan counting the *cri* sound. "Time for cookies and milk!" she says.

"Yay!" says Ivan.

"Oh, look!" says Grandma. "It's a rainbow." The rainbow goes from the house to the forest. It has many colors: red, orange, yellow, blue and green. The rainbow is beautiful. Grandma, Grandpa and Ivan watch the rainbow. It disappears and they go inside.

"Cookies and milk for everyone," says Grandma. She gives Ivan a warm chocolate cookie.

"Not for me," says Grandpa. "I want tea."

"Why tea?" says Grandma. She has two milks in her hand.

"I'm feeling **under the weather**," says Grandpa. He laughs. Ivan and Grandma laugh with him.

CONCLUSION

You did it!

You finished a whole book in a brand new language. That in and of itself is quite the accomplishment, isn't it?

Congratulate yourself on time well spent and a job well done. Now that you've finished the book, you have familiarized yourself with over 500 new vocabulary words, comprehended the heart of 3 short stories, and listened to loads of dialogue unfold, all without going anywhere!

Charlemagne said "To have another language is to possess a second soul." After immersing yourself in this book, you are broadening your horizons and opening a whole new path for yourself.

Have you thought about how much you know now that you did not know before? You've learned everything from how to greet and how to express your emotions to basics like colors and place words. You can tell time and ask question. All without opening a schoolbook. Instead, you've cruised through fun, interesting stories and possibly listened to them as well.

Perhaps before you weren't able to distinguish meaning when you listened to Spanish. If you used the audiobook, we bet you can now pick out meanings and words when you hear someone speaking. Regardless, we are sure you have taken an important step to being more fluent. You are well on your way!

Best of all, you have made the essential step of distinguishing in your mind the idea that most often hinders people studying a new language. By approaching Spanish through our short stories and dialogs, instead of formal lessons with just grammar and vocabulary, you are no longer in the 'learning' mindset. Your approach is much more similar to an osmosis, focused on speaking and using the language, which is the end goal, after all!

So, what's next?

This is just the first of five books, all packed full of short stories and dialogs, covering essential, everyday Spanish that will ensure you master the basics. You can find the rest of the books in the series, as well as a whole host of other resources, at LearnLikeNatives.com. Simply add the book to your library to take the next step in your language learning journey. If you are ever in need of new ideas or direction, refer to our 'Speak Like a Native' eBook, available to you for free at LearnLikeNatives.com, which clearly outlines practical steps you can take to continue learning any language you choose.

We also encourage you to get out into the real world and practice your Spanish. You have a leg up on most beginners, after all—instead of pure textbook learning, you have been absorbing the sound and soul of the language. Do not underestimate the foundation you have built reviewing the chapters of this book. Remember, no one feels 100% confident when they speak with a native speaker in another language.

One of the coolest things about being human is connecting with others. Communicating with someone in their own language is a wonderful gift. Knowing the language turns you into a local and opens up your world. You will see the reward of learning languages for many years to come, so keep that practice up!. Don't let your fears stop you from taking the chance to use your Spanish. Just give it a try, and remember that you will make mistakes. However, these mistakes will teach you so much, so view every single one as a small victory! Learning is growth.

Don't let the quest for learning end here! There is so much you can do to continue the learning process in an organic way, like you did with this book. Add another book from Learn Like a Native to your library. Listen to Spanish talk radio. Watch some of the great Spanish films. Put on the latest

CD from Rosalia. Take salsa lessons in Spanish. Whatever you do, don't stop because every little

step you take counts towards learning a new language, culture, and way of communicating.

www.LearnLikeNatives.com

Learn Like a Native is a revolutionary **language education brand** that is taking the linguistic world by storm. Forget boring grammar books that never get you anywhere, Learn Like a Native teaches you languages in a fast and fun way that actually works!

As an international, multichannel, language learning platform, we provide **books, audio guides and eBooks** so that you can acquire the knowledge you need, swiftly and easily.

Our **subject-based learning**, structured around real-world scenarios, builds your conversational muscle and ensures you learn the content most relevant to your requirements. Discover our tools at *LearnLikeNatives.com*.

When it comes to learning languages, we've got you covered!